CUBE
BOOK

WHITE STAR PUBLISHERS

EDITED BY

VALERIA MANFERTO DE FABIANIS

text by

ALBERTO BERTOLAZZI

GIORGIO FERRERO

FEDERICA ROMAGNOLI

graphic design

CLARA ZANOTTI

graphic layout

STEFANIA COSTANZO

editorial coordination

GIADA FRANCIA

translation

YOLANDA RILLORTA

© 2008 EDIZIONI WHITE STAR S.R.L.
VIA CANDIDO SASSONE, 24
13100 VERCELLI - ITALY
WWW.WHITESTAR.IT

Revised edition, 2011

- Sydney's Opera House with its white sails.

ISBN 978-88-544-0599-8
REPRINTS:
2 3 4 5 6 16 15 14 13 12
Printed in China

CONTENTS

WONDERS OF THE WORLD

1 • At the border between Argentina and Brazil, the waters of the Iguazù river form impressive falls.

2-3 • Bora Bora, with its turquoise lagoon, one of most acclaimed islands of French Polynesia.

4-5 • The faces of Avalokiteshvara bodhisattva depicted on the sides of the Bayon Tower in Angkor Thom.

6-7 • The peaks of the Catinaccio Dolomites, turned pink in the setting sun.

8-9 • The statue of Christ the Redeemer dominates the bay and the city of Rio De Janeiro.

13 • The army of terracotta warriors of Xi'an, discovered in 1974 in the tomb of the first Chinese Emperor.

14-15 • The Bilbao Guggenheim Museum designed by Architect Frank O. Gehry.

16-17 • The dome of the Basilica of St Peter in Rome, designed by Michelangelo.

Introduction

by Giorgio Ferrero

IN LISBON ON 7 JULY 2007, THE NEW "SEVEN WONDERS OF THE WORLD" WERE PROCLAIMED. THEY WERE CHOSEN FROM A WIDE RANGE OF CANDIDATES AND MILLIONS OF PEOPLE VOTED FOR THE CHOICES THROUGH THE MOST MODERN MEANS OF COMMUNICATION. THE FINAL RESULTS MAY BE DEBATABLE – AND SO ALSO MAY BE THE CRITERIA FOR THE INITIAL SCREENING – BUT THE ORIGINALITY OF THE INITIATIVE LAUNCHED BY THE ECLECTIC SWISS-CANADIAN DIRECTOR BERNARD WEBER TESTIFIES TO THE RELEVANCE OF THE WONDERS OF THE WORLD THEME. IT ALSO DRAWS ATTENTION TO THE NEED TO SAFEGUARD THE NATURAL LEGACY AND THE ARCHAEOLOGICAL AND ARCHITECTONIC HERITAGE OF OUR PLANET, A NEED WHICH TODAY AROUSES GREAT INTEREST AND CONCERN THROUGHOUT SOCIETY.

- The majestic Taj Mahal mausoleum, built by Muslim Emperor Shah Jahan in memory of his wife and today a symbol of India.

Introduction

AS YOU LEAF THROUGH THE PAGES OF THIS BOOK YOU WILL SURELY REALIZE THAT IT IS PRACTICALLY IMPOSSIBLE, IF NOT USELESS, TO DRAFT A CLASSIFICATION OR LIMIT TO A MERE SEVEN THE MOST SPECTACULAR AND AMAZING PLACES, LANDSCAPES, MONUMENTS AND WORKS ON OUR PLANET. THE NUMBER AND TYPES OF PRECIOUS TREASURES SCATTERED ALL OVER THE SURFACE OF THE GLOBE ARE SUCH THAT EACH SELECTION ALSO IMPLIES A PAINFUL EXCLUSION OF OTHER WORTHY CANDIDATES. WE MOST PROBABLY HAVE NOT STOPPED TO CONSIDER THE FACT, BUT TODAY WE KNOW OF AND ADMIRE A MUCH GREATER NUMBER OF WONDERS THAN THOSE THAT WERE KNOWN ONLY A FEW CENTURIES AGO. EXPLORATION, ARCHAEOLOGICAL RESEARCH AND NEW TECHNOLOGIES HAVE ALLOWED US TO REVEAL HIDDEN NATURAL EDENS, AND DISCOVER

Introduction

UNEXPECTED TRACES OF THE PAST OR CREATE NEW AND EX-CEPTIONAL WORKS OF GENIUS.

PARADOXICALLY HOWEVER, ALTHOUGH DISTANCES HAVE BEEN OVERCOME AND THE POSSIBILITIES TO KNOW AND EN-JOY HAVE BECOME INFINITE, SOME OF THE WONDERS OF THE WORLD FACE GREATER THREATS OF DESTRUCTION TODAY THAN EVER BEFORE. THE WORKS WHICH NATURE MOLDED DURING THE COURSE OF MILLENNIA ARE AT RISK OF DISAP-PEARING FOREVER BECAUSE OF THE HAZARDOUS AND IN-CONSIDERATE DECISIONS CONTEMPORARY MAN HAS MADE. THERE HAVE BEEN, HOWEVER, MANY INITIATIVES TO SAFE-GUARD AND PRESERVE THE MOST THREATENED SITES – THE MOST EVIDENT AMONG WHICH ARE PROBABLY REPRE-SENTED BY UNESCO'S LIST OF WORLD HERITAGE SITES –

Introduction

BUT THE CHALLENGE IS SURELY STILL FAR FROM BEING WON. THROUGH THE SPLENDID IMAGES IN THIS VOLUME, WE WANTED TO PRESENT A SELECTION OF THE WORLD'S MOST FASCINATING AND ASTOUNDING PLACES, WITH THE PRIMARY AIM OF OFFERING JOY TO OUR EYES, BUT ALSO IN THE HOPE OF EVOKING DEEP REFLECTION.

SO LET US ENCOMPASS DURING THIS JOURNEY THROUGH PLANET EARTH'S NATURAL WONDERS THE MOST FAMOUS AND THE MOST VISITED – SUCH AS THE GRAND NORTH AMERICAN PARKS AND THE AFRICAN SAVANNA – BUT WITHOUT OMITTING LESS FAMOUS AND LESS VISITED SITES SUCH AS THE GREAT FROZEN EXPANSES OF THE POLES OR THE LUXURIANT EQUATORIAL FORESTS. PREPARE YOURSELF TO VISIT INSPIRING ARCHAEOLOGICAL REMAINS IN THE DESERT SANDS OR TROPICAL

Introduction

LAGOONS IN UNINHABITED LANDS OR IN THE MIDST OF THE BUILDINGS OF MODERN CITIES – THE MEN OF THE PAST HAVE LEFT THEM TO US AS A SIGN OF THEIR PASSAGE. AND FINALLY, ENJOY REDISCOVERING THE COUNTLESS ARCHITECTONIC MASTERPIECES – FROM THE PLACES OF WORSHIP TO THE SEATS OF POWER, AND FROM THE GRAND SKYSCRAPERS TO THE FUTURISTIC MUSEUMS OF THE NEW MILLENNIUM. THEY ARE ALL AROUND US, KEEPING IN STRIDE WITH US IN OUR DAILY LIVES. GET READY TO SAVOR IN A SINGLE EVOCATIVELY ILLUSTRATED JOURNEY ALL THE INCREDIBLE WONDERS OF OUR ONE AND ONLY PLANET!

24-25 • Pharaoh Ramesses II commissioned the building of the rock-cut temple of Abu Simbel in Nubia, Egypt.

26-27 • A group of Antarctic penguins sheltering from a sea storm.

TREASURES

of the

PAST

GIORGIO FERRERO

- The Pyramid of Menkaure at Giza, surrounded by three satellite pyramids, all burial sites of queens.

INTRODUCTION Treasures of the Past

Toward the end of the 2nd century b.c., when the poet, Antipater of Sidon, composed an epigram dedicated to the seven wonders of the world, he referred to existing monuments or to those that had only recently disappeared, but the fame of which was still vivid and deeply rooted. He certainly could not have imagined that time, calamities and the destructive fury of man would have obliterated all those marvelous works, preserving only the most ancient: the pyramids of Giza in Egypt. These pyramids of the pharaonic civilization stand today as the most outstanding symbol of the archaeological wonders scattered over the panorama of different continents of the world, the tangible mark of hu-

INTRODUCTION Treasures of the Past

MAN GENIUS EXPRESSED OVER CENTURIES AND MILLENNIA. ETYMOLOGICALLY DEFINED AS THE "STUDY OF ANCIENT CUL-TURES", ARCHAEOLOGY INVESTIGATES THE TRACES LEFT TO US BY ANCIENT CIVILIZATIONS, THEIR HISTORY, RELIGION, BELIEFS, THE ASPECTS OF DAILY LIFE, AND THE ARTISTIC AND ARCHITEC-TONIC WORKS OF THOSE WHO PRECEDED US. THIS RESEARCH CONTINUES TO FIRE OUR EMOTIONS AND AMAZE US, EMBODY-ING IN THE FINAL ANALYSIS AN IN-DEPTH STUDY OF OUR OWN SELVES, OUR PAST AND OUR ORIGINS. THE PATIENT WORK OF ARCHAEOLOGISTS AND THE FORTUNATE FINDINGS OF EXPLOR-ERS OR EVEN SIMPLE WAYFARERS HAVE ALLOWED US TO DIS-COVER – AND CONTINUE TO MAKE US DISCOVER – ASPECTS AND WONDERS OF THE ANCIENT WORLD THAT OTHERWISE WOULD HAVE BEEN LOST FOREVER. THIS VOLUME TRACES THE

Treasures of the Past

Introduction

REMAINS OF THE MEDITERRANEAN CULTURES, FROM GREEK AND ROMAN MONUMENTAL WORKS TO THOSE OF PHARAONIC EGYPT, AND MOVES ON TO THE ANCIENT CITIES OF THE NEAR EAST AND TO THE TEMPLES AND SITES OF INDIAN RELIGIOUS GROUPS; IT ALSO TAKES NOTE OF THE MONUMENTS OF AN-CIENT EMPIRES OF THE FAR EAST – WITHOUT NEGLECTING THE IMPORTANT HERITAGE OF THE PRE-COLUMBIAN CIVILIZATIONS OF AMERICA. THE SPLENDID PICTURES CHOSEN TO ILLUSTRATE THE WORLD-ENCOMPASSING *WONDERS OF ARCHAEOLOGY* SUPPLY US WITH AN EFFECTIVE AND LIVELY RECORD OF WHAT THE PEOPLE OF ANCIENT TIMES HAVE HANDED DOWN TO US AS A CULTURAL HERITAGE AND AS A WAY OF THINKING ABOUT AND CELEBRATING OUR HUMANITY.

- Machu Picchu, the legendary city of the Incas in the Urubamba Valley, overshadowed by Mt Huayna Picchu .

34 ● Each of these three inner-circle strutures within the Stonehenge monument has two massive uprights and a megalithic lintel.

35 ● The Stonehenge megalithic site is believed to have been constructed and reconstructed between 3000 and 1600 BC.

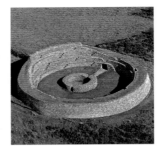

**The Forts
of Ireland**

36 • Ireland and its minor isles preserve countless remains of prehistoric monuments. From the upper left: Newgrange, Cahergal, Leacanbuaile, Dún Aengus, Dún Chonchúir, Dún Eochla.

37 • The oval stone fort of Dún Aengus overlooks the cliffs of the Island of Inishmore, Ireland.

The aqueduct bridge of Gard near Nîmes (Nemausus), in France, was commissioned by Agrippa, father-in-law of Augustus, and is formed by three tiers of arches.

40-41 • The Arena of Verona, Italy, is one of the best preserved Roman amphitheaters. It was built with Veronese marble in the 1st century AD.

42-43 • The Imperial Forum quarter in Rome, Italy, was the public square and center of the public affairs of the vast Roman Empire.

44 • The great dome of the Pantheon, in Rome, decorated with five concentric rows of lacunars culminating in an oeil-de-boeuf opening.

45 • The Pantheon, temple dedicated to various divinities, was commissioned by Agrippa, father-in-law of Augustus, but was completely rebuilt during Emperor Hadrian's time.

46 • The Maritime Theater is one of the most original buildings at Hadrian's Villa, Tivoli, Italy. It includes a nymphaeum where Hadrian loved to hold his meditative retreats.

46-47 • Hadrian's Villa was chosen by the Emperor as his private residence and it manifested his great passion for art.

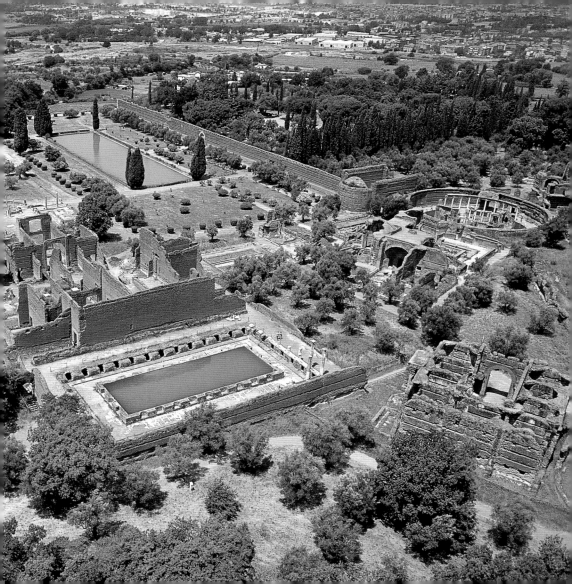

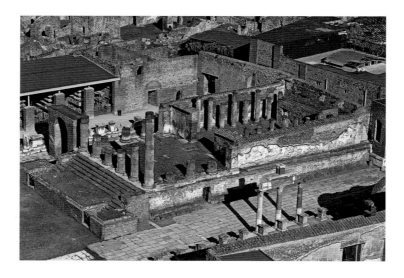

48 • The Temple of Jupiter in the Forum of Pompeii, Italy was a center for worship dedicated to the three divinities Jupiter, Juno and Minerva.

49 • The eruption of Vesuvius buried Pompeii in lava, but also caused its preservation through later centuries.

50 ● The atrium and tablinum of the House of Marcus Lucretius Fronto, decorated with refined polychrome paint.

51 ● Villa of Mysteries outside the walls of Pompeii, famous for its stunning frescoes representing the Dionysian mysteries.

52-53 • In the 6th century BC,
distinctive square tombs
appeared in the Etruscan
necropolis of Cerveteri, Italy. They
became known as "dice tombs."

53 • The graves of the
Necropolis of Banditaccia
at Cerveteri acted as burial sites
for entire Entruscan aristocratic
families of the 7th century BC.

A banquet scene is depicted on the back wall of the Leopardi burial site in Tarquinia, a typical example of Etruscan funerary iconography dating back to the 5th century BC.

56-57 • The Temple of Segesta, in Sicily, is one of the best examples of a Doric temple in Magna Graecia. It is unfinished and has no cella.

57 • The Segesta Theater blends with the landscape of the hill on which it was built, a site purposely chosen for its acoustic features.

58-59 • The Concordia of Agrigento, in Sicily, is one of the most harmonious temples of the Doric Age.

59 • The Greek theater at Syracuse, in Sicily, was built during the Hellenistic Age and restructured during the reign of Augustus.

● The Parthenon, a
Doric temple of elegant
proportions dedicated
to the Goddess Athena,
overlooks the Acropolis
of Athens, in Greece.

62 • The city of Mycenae stands on a steep hill soaring over the Argos plain in Greece, protected by an impressive wall.

63 • The Lion Gate was the entrance to the city of Mycenae. Its name derives from the triangular plate depicting two lions carved in stone relief.

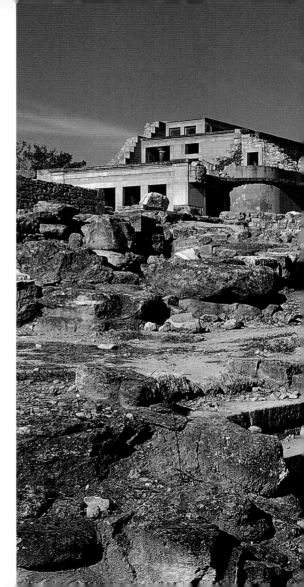

64 ● The southern propylaeum of the Palace of Knossos, in Crete, are polychromatic paintings depicting processions of youth bearing their offerings.

64-65 ● At the central entrance of Knossos's group of palaces a terraced bastion depicts the capture of a bull.

66 • In the city of Voubilis, in the province of Mauretania, Northern Africa, Emperor Caracalla built a triumphal arch with a single fornix.

67 • Dazzling mosaics adorn the floors of the House of Dionysus and the Four Seasons in Volubilis.

68-69 • The magnificent stage of the Theater at Sabratha, near Tripoli, Lybia, with its three stories of columns.

69 • A colonnade partly obstructs the view of the outer wall of the Sabratha theater, lined with arches.

70 • The market (*macellum*) of Leptis Magna with its two round buildings (*tholoi*) in the center.

71 • A small arch built by Emperor Trajan on the *decumanus* of Leptis Magna.

Saharan Rock Art

72 ● The solid blocks of rock in the Sahara desert form an open-air museum because of their countless examples of rock art.

73 ● This rock engraving of Wadi Mathendush, in the Sahara Desert in Libya, is also known as the "Wadi Mathendush cats."

74-75 ● A herd of giraffes engraved on the rock of Wadi Mathsendu in Libya: a fine example of Saharan rock art.

A characteristic Step Pyramid stands out in the Egyptian site of Saqqara. It was the funeral site of King Djoser of the 3rd Dynasty.

● The 4th Dynasty pharaohs, Khufu Khafre and Menkaure built their pyramids on the plain of Giza; they have always been considered architectural wonders.

80 • The Sphinx of Giza is one of the most renowned and enigmatic monuments of ancient Egypt.

81 • The face of the Sphinx probably reproduced the facial features of the King who built it: Khafre.

● The funerary temples
of Queen Hatshepsut
and Pharaoh
Montuhotep II stand at
the foot of the rocky
amphitheater
of Deir el-Bahari.

A portico marked by gigantic Osirid statues looking out on the second court yard of Ramesses, leading to the hypostyle hall of the temple.

The funerary chamber of Queen Nefertari's tomb in the Valley of Queens is characterized by four pillars that seem to sustain the starry sky painted on the ceiling.

● The semi-rock temple
of Wadi es-Sebua,
in Egyptian Nubia, was
built by Ramesses to honor
the gods Amun and
Re-Horakhte.

90 • The figure of the god Re-Horakhte is carved above the entrance of the great temple of
Abu Simbel, between two statues of the pharaoh bearing offerings.

91 • Engraved in Nubian stone, four gigantic statues of Ramesses II on his throne mark
out the façade of the great temple of Abu Simbel.

92-93 • The Herodium is the fortress-residence and mausoleum built by Herod, the king of Judah, south of Jerusalem in Israel.

93 • Beit Shean, in Israel was an important city during the Hellenistic-Roman period thanks to its strategic position in the Jordan Valley.

94-95 • The fortress of Masada, built by King Herod on an isolated rock, was the seat of a bloody and tragic Jewish revolt against the Romans.

96-97 • The profile of the rock temple of the El Deir "Monastery" emerging from the cliff face of Petra, in Jordan.

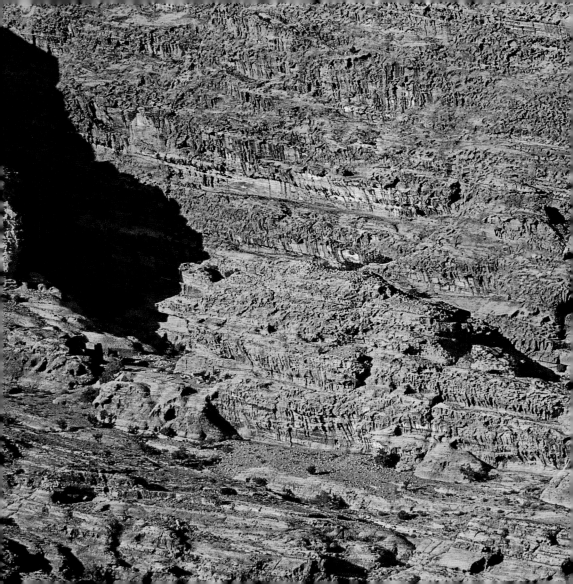

98 ● The façade of the temple of the El Deir at Petra portrays a mixture of curved and straight lines that transcend the classic laws of architecture.

99 ● The façade of the Khasné, a magnificent rock tomb in Petra, appears at the end of the narrow ravine known as the Siq.

100 • The 13th-century Ayyubid
fortress seen against the
background of the Street
of the Columns, in Palmyra, Syria.

100-101 • An three-fornix arch
built during the Severan age
introduces the long Street of the
Columns, in Palmyra.

102-103 • On the summit of Nemrut Dag in the Taurus mountain range in Turkey, Antiochus I of Commagene built his own mausoleum.

103 • Gigantic statues in stone lie on the terraces of the Tomb-Temple of Nemrut Dag.

104-105 • The Palace of Darius at Persepolis stands on a platform with large relief decorations.

106 • The reliefs of Apadana, in Persepolis, depict a parade of soldiers with lances.

107 • A lion attacking a bull, a recurrent theme of the reliefs in Persepolis.

The Great Stupa at Sanchi

108 • Sensational reliefs adorn the Great Stupa at Sanchi, one of the most ancient sites of Buddhist worship in India.

109 • The entrance to the Great Stupa at Sanchi with majestic portals bearing relief decorations on its architraves.

110 • The stairway leads to a balustrade and a pathway which divides the central body of the Great Stupa at Sanchi.

110-111 • The Great Stupa of Sanchi is surrounded by a stone wall that leads to the grand portals.

112 ● The Wat Phra Si Sanphet was
a great temple of Ayutthaya, used
by the Thai kings as a royal chapel

112-113 ● The Wat Chaiwathanaram of
Ayutthaya drew architectonic inspiration
from the Khmer monuments in Angkor.

● Inside grotto 26 of Ajanta, India, there is an engraved portrait of Buddha during his ascent to Nirvana.

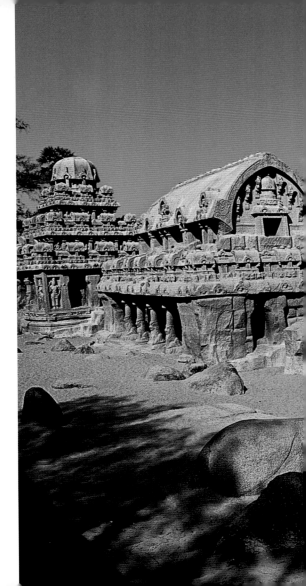

116 • The temple of Riva in Mahabalipuram, near the coast of Tamil Nadu, with its two square towers.

116-117 • Five monolithic temples were carved out as procession chariots for the gods in the mass of rock of Mahabalipuram.

118-119 • At the entrance of one of the temples of Khajuraho, in India, stands the statue of a lion being enticed by a prince, symbol of the Chandelas Dynasty.

119 • The Kandariya Mahadeva Temple of Khajuraho is one of the biggest and the best preserved among the temples of medieval India.

120-121 • Over 3100 miles (5000 km) of walls and towers make up the Great Wall of China, the world's biggest defense system.

121 • A stretch of the Great Wall weaves its way over the Hebei mountain peaks.

122-123 • Rows of terracotta warriors buried in the pit discovered near the mausoleum of the Chnese Emperor, Qin Shi Huangdi, in Xi'an.

124 • The faces and the armored suits of the Chinese terracotta army of Xi'an portray impressive real-life features.

125 • The statues of the infantry of the Qin Shi Huangdi Army are accompanied by their horse-driven carts.

● Sculptures of sacred dancers (*apsaras*)
and divinities (*devatas*) decorate the wide
walls of Angkor Wat, in Cambodia, a vast
temple complex dating to the Khmer era.

128 ● The Cambodian jungle wraps around the ancient Khmer buildings, in some instances, completely absorbing them.

128-129 ● The entrance gate to the city of Angkor Thom is flanked by rows of kings and demons carrying a snake.

130-131 ● The ruins of the numberless temples stand out in the plain around Pagan, ancient capital of the Burmese Empire.

132 ● The great stone statues of Easter Island are known as Moai and were built in rows on a enormous platform called Ahu.

133 ● Today a great number of Moai statues lie in pieces on the slopes of the hills on Easter Island.

134 • The Cliff Palace, in Mesa Verde National Park, Colorado, has the biggest cluster of Anasazi-culture rock settlements.

135 • The Anasazi Cliff Palace site has multistory buildings and several large circular rooms (*kivas*) used for religious rites.

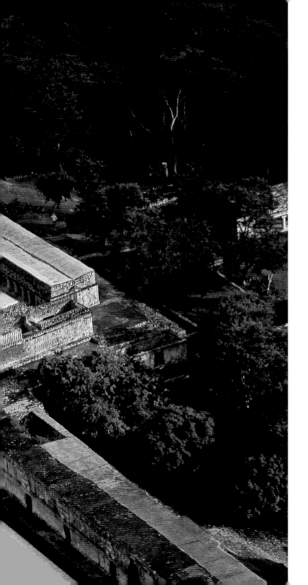

136-137 • The Pyramid of the Magician in Uxmal, Mexico, presents an outstanding cone structure.

137 • The "Nunnery" of Uxmal consists of parallelepiped constructions with elaborate geometrical mosaics in stone.

138-139 ● The Pyramid of El Castillo in Chichén Itzá, in Mexico, was dedicated to the feathered snake Kukulkan.

139 ● From the Temple of the Warriors of Chichén Itzá, one can see the pyramid of El Castillo.

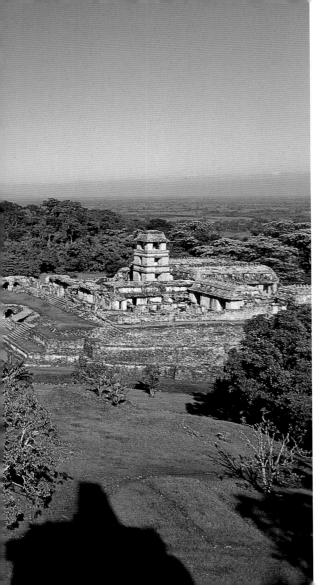

140-141 ● The Maya
site of Palenque,
in Mexico, owes
it splendor to its
monuments, the work
of King Pacal and
his sons.

142-143 ● The ruins
on the post-classical
site of Tulum in Mexico,
directly facing the
crystalline waters
of the eastern coast
of the Yucatán.

144 • The Pyramid of the Moon stands at the end of the Street of the Dead, an axis road of Teotihuacan.

145 • Heads of feathered snakes engraved in a variety of ways, ornate one of the main temples of Teotihuacan.

146 • The summit of the Maya pyramid, known as Temple IV, stands out from the tropical forest that surrounds the ruins of Tikal, in Guatemala.

147 • The Pyramid of the Lost World goes back to the most ancient era of the Maya site of Tikal.

148-149 • Overlooking the central square of Tikal is the northern Acropolis (on the left) with the pyramid known as Temple I (on the right).

150 • A characteristic feature of the Nazca culture of southern Peru are the huge glyphs traced out on the land.

150-151 • Incised in the soil but fully visible only from the sky, these works of the Nazca people are sometimes ascribed to the "aliens."

152-153 • The Cyclopean walls of Sacsahuaman, near Cuzco, in Peru, were part of a religious complex dedicated by the Incas to the Sun God.

154-155 • Machu Picchu, due to its position, hidden among the Andean peaks, was discovered only in 1911.

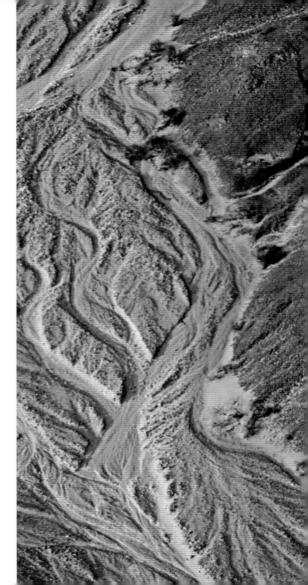

On the NATURE of the UNIVERSE

ALBERTO BERTOLAZZI

- The Nuptse (25,791 ft/7861 m), in Nepal, as viewed from Kalapattar peak.

INTRODUCTION On the Nature of the Universe

IN THE BEGINNING ALL WAS PRISTINE NATURE, AND THE BEAUTIFUL AND THE UGLY WERE UNKNOWN QUALITIES. AT THE DAWNING OF TIME, HUMANKIND HAD TO ADDRESS OTHER MATTERS: SURVIVAL AND ABOVE ALL, REPRODUCTION OF THE SPECIES. THE LOSS OF NATURE AND THE AWARENESS OF ITS WONDERS CAME LATER, WHEN HUNGER AND THIRST HAD BEEN QUENCHED. HUMANKIND TODAY KNOWS THAT NATURE IS A PRECIOUS GIFT, A RESOURCE WHICH IS NOT ETERNAL, A JEWEL CASE NOT ONLY TO BE ADMIRED BUT TO BE CONTEMPLATED WITH RESPECT. AS KNOWLEDGE SPREADS THIS AWARENESS GROWS, ENABLING US TO AVOID REPEATING SOME OF THE ERRORS OF THE PAST. NOT TOO LONG AGO, JUST THE THOUGHT OF CREATION MADE US LOSE OUR

INTRODUCTION On the Nature of the Universe

WAY IN A DREAMY PURSUIT OF OF ICONS. WE ENDED UP BY CONFUSING REALITY WITH POSTCARD IMAGES: THE AMAZON FOREST, MT EVEREST, THE AUSTRALIAN CORAL REEFS, THE ERG DUNES OF TUNISIA, THE GRAND CANYON, THE IGUAZÚ WATERFALLS, THE RIFT VALLEY . . . A TOUR OF THE WONDERS WITH COMPULSORY STOPOVERS IN NATURE'S GCLDEN SHOWCASES.

IF ON ONE HAND, BY EXALTING NATURE WE CONTRIBUTE TO INTENSIFYING OUR FEELINGS OF ASTONISHMENT, ON THE OTHER HAND THIS INSTILLS AN UNFOUNDED CONVICTION THAT THE ENVIRONMENT IS ABSOLUTELY SELF-GENERATING. BUT THIS IS NOT SO: NATURE IS SUFFERING FROM HUMANKIND'S AGGRESSIVENESS AND NONE OF THE WONDERS OF THE PLANET CAN BE DECLARED SAFE. WHAT CAN

INTRODUCTION On the Nature of the Universe

WE DO? IN THIS VOLUME WE CHOSE TO SHOW THE MAS-
TERPIECES OF HUMANKIND AND THOSE OF NATURE
ALONGSIDE ONE ANOTHER. IT IS A SIGN OF FAITH IN THE
GENIUS OF HUMANKIND, BUT IT IS ALSO OUR WAY OF UN-
DERLINING THE SENSATIONAL POWER OF BEAUTY. JUST A
QUICK GLANCE AT THESE EXTRAORDINARY PICTURES
WOULD BE ENOUGH TO MAKE US GAUGE THE MAGNIFI-
CENT TREASURES OF OUR PLANET AND THE SERIOUS DAN-
GERS THREATENING THEM. SOME EXAMPLES: POLAR PACK
ICE THAT COULD SHRINK BECAUSE OF GLOBAL WARMING;
THE MAJESTIC, FANTASTIC FLIGHT OF EAGLES, NOW SADLY
CONFINED TO NATURAL PARKS; THE AMAZING COLLECTIVE
ORGANISMS SUCH AS THE BANKS OF THE BLUE MAOMAO
THAT COME TO LIVE, FEED, GROW, REPRODUCE AND DIE IN

INTRODUCTION On the Nature of the Universe

GROUPS IN THE OPEN SEA OFF THE COASTS OF NEW ZEALAND, AND ARE NOW SUFFERING FROM THE POLLUTED OCEANIC WATERS; THE QUETZAL, THE MYTHICAL SOUTH AMERICAN BIRD WITH ITS RAINBOW PLUMAGE, ALMOST EXTINCT BECAUSE OF FEATHER HUNTERS . . . BUT WE SHALL STOP HERE.

WHAT YOU WILL SEE IN THIS VOLUME IS NOT A FORMAL PROTEST, BUT A CATALOG OF BEAUTY WHICH WILL ASTONISH YOU AND PROVE THAT IN THE END, FRAGMENTS OF PARADISE LOST CAN BE FOUND EVERYWHERE: IN THE FLOODPLAINS OF THE OKAVANGO RIVER, ONE OF THE RICHEST NATURAL RESERVES OF THE PLANET, BORN THROUGH A TRICK OF DESTINY; IN THE AURORA BOREALIS WHICH PAINTS THE POLAR SKIES GREEN, RED AND BLUE; IN

On the Nature of the Universe
Introduction

THE LEOPARDS, PERFECT HUNTING AND RACING MACHINES; IN THE ISLANDS OF THAILAND'S PHANGNGA BAY, DUG OUT BY THE TIDES; IN THE ANNAPURNA CIRCLE, FRUIT OF TECTONIC POWER; AND IN THE ABYSMAL COLCA CANYON, CHISELED OUT BY THE WATERS OF THE ANDES. . . .

LET US ENJOY THIS VOLUME OF SPECTACULAR IMAGES, CONSCIOUS OF OUR RESPONSIBILITY AND OUR PRIVILEGE: WE ALONE IN THE ENTIRE UNIVERSE CAN GRASP THE MEANING OF THESE WONDERS.

163 • The Grand Prismatic Spring is a geological phenomenon in the heart of Yellowstone National Park, Wyoming, U.S.A.

164-165 • A primordial volcanic landscape leading to the Mydalsjökull glaciers in Iceland.

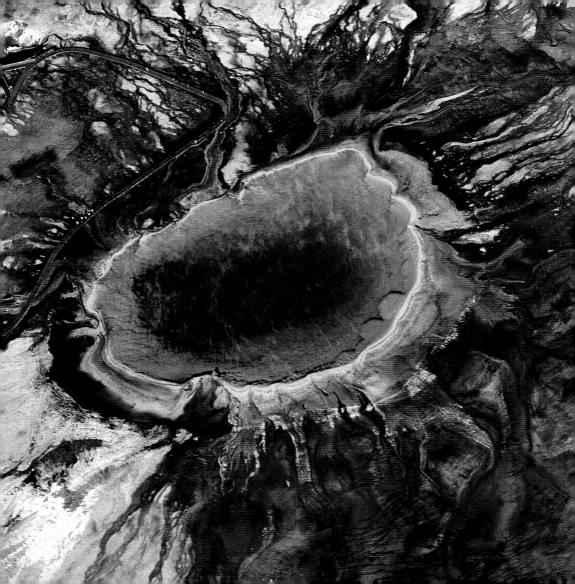

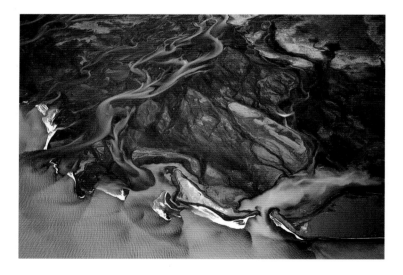

166 • The Hvitá River flows into the Hvítárvatn Lake in Iceland, creating thousands of twisting rivulets of water, colored by the mineral sediments it carries.

167 • The Thorsa River, without a well-defined river bed, flows down the glaciers of Hofsjökull in Iceland in an interwoven pattern of canals.

168 • The aurora borealis weaves fantastic patterns of light in the sky above Iceland's Halendi Islands.

169 • The aurora borealis is an electromagnetic phenomenon typical of the Polar circles.

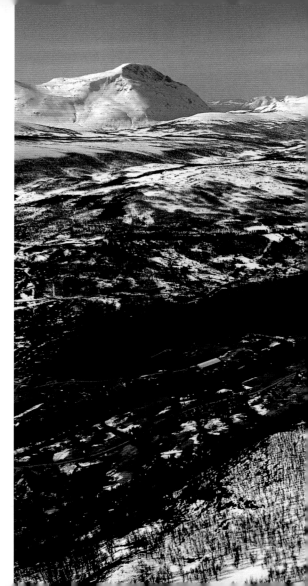

170 • Seas and glaciers meet in the Ofotfjorden fiord, in Norway.

170-171 • The long tongue of salt of the Vagsfjorden pushes its way into the coast of Troms.

Frozen trees covered with snow stick out like sculptures from the mantle of snow covering Riisitunturi National Park, Finland, just below the Arctic Circle.

174 • An idyllic view of the Oulanka National Park in Finland.

175 • The lakes and peat bogs of glacial origin of Finland are ecological niches that are unique in an essential habitat for the survival of rich sedentary or migratory birdlife.

176-177 and 178-179 ● Extending along the border with Russia, Finland's Oulanka National Park safeguards 104 sq. miles (217 sq. km) of Nordic habitat and conifer trees traversed by heterogeneous streams that are torrential and with falls in the highland zones but slow and sandy in the plains.

180-181 ● The Scandinavian autumn offers these extraordinary colors in the beech forests that characterize the southern strip of Lapland, the region extending over the Norwegian, Swedish, Finnish and Russian border region.

182-183 ● The Aran Islands, in Galway Bay, on Ireland's west coast, are three green pearls of great romantic beauty, a source of inspiration for writers and artists.

184 • The town of Keswick overlooking Derwentwater, one of the lakes that form part of England's enchanting Lake District.

185 • Coniston Water, like all the other bodies of water in the Lake District, is a perfect example of a basin of glacial origin.

186-187 • Winter's end in Berchtesgaden: the ice around the rivulets is starting to melt, whereas the banks and treetops are still white with snow. This part of Bavaria, in Germany, offer awe-inspiring views that have remained unchanged throughout the centuries.

188-189 • White cliffs that rise from the sea, arches excavated from the waves: these features mark the Norman coast at Étretat, France.

● Provence is known for its
lavender, an aromatic plant
traditionally cultivated in a large
part of the territory, inundating
the summer landscape with
its violet color.

● Les Calanques, near Marseilles in France, extend for about 12.5 miles (20 km) toward the sea, tracing a jagged coastline with deep green bays and white cliffs.

- The Calanques de Piana area is a bizarre geological formation located south of the city of Porto, Corsica. The red granite rocks, rising about 1312 ft (400 m) above sea level, are listed as a World Heritage Site by UNESCO.

The Bernese Oberland, also
known as the Jungfrau Region,
is probably the most spectacular
focal point of the Swiss Alps.
The Jungfrau, Mönch and
the Eiger are a trio of
incomparable beauty.

● To many, it is the
most beautiful
mountain worldwide.
Italy and Switzerland vie
for it, given that it
stands right at their
frontiers: but the
Matterhorn, a splendid
pyramid of rocks
and glaciers soaring
14,692 ft (4478 m),
is the highest peak
in Europe.

200 • The Gnifetti Peak (14,941 ft/4554 meters), a summit of Monte Rosa, Italy, bathed in dawn light.

200-201 • Capanna Margherita at the top of Monte Rosa is the highest mountain refuge in Europe (14,957 ft/4559 m).

202-203 • The White Valley descends from the peaks of the massif. The summit is seen on the left (15,781 ft/4810 m), on the right the Aiguille du Midi (12,605 ft/3842 m).

204 ● The flying buttresses in the Brenta Group (10,410 ft/3173 m), in Italy, remind one of a Gothic cathedral.

205 ● The Marmolada (10,968 ft/3343 m), Italy, is an awe-inspiring wall of rock marking the border of Venice and Trento provinces. It saw dramatic action in World War One.

206-207 ● Mt Etna (10,902 ft/3323 m) is Europe's highest volcano. Its immense mass dominates the city of Catania and is visible from a great part of northeastern Sicily.

208-209 ● Vulcano Island, one
of the Eolie Islands, is the result
of age-old volcanic activity.

209 ● Stromboli Island, in the
Aeolian Sea, owes its typical
conical form to the volcano
that created it.

210-211 ● Rabbit Island,
off Lampedusa, offers one of the
most ravishing coastal stretches
of the region.

212-213 and 213 • Algarve, the southwesternmost region of Portugal, is its principal tourist attraction. These pictures explain the reasons behind this fact. They were taken near Sagres, a vast stretch of beaches with the most incredible natural landscapes.

214-215 • Zante (Zákinthos) is the northernmost Greek island in the Ionian Sea. Its luxuriant vegetation, white beaches and crystal sea make it a real paradise; it is also the haven for sea turtles that come ashore to deposit their eggs on the beach.

● Elinda Bay, on the
island of Chios, is
a fantastic area
for sailboat enthusiasts
and an ideal habitat for
Mediterranean fauna
and flora.

The dark color of the rocks extending toward the sea near Agadir, Morocco, confirms the age and volcanic origin of this stretch of North Africa's Atlantic Coast.

220-221 ● The cliffs of the southern coast in the region of El Aaiún, Morocco, are characterized by stratified rock, eroded by ocean waves.

222-223 ● The Gezira Tawira coral reefs, between Sinai and Egypt's Red Sea, display strange concentric circles centering upon higher land.

224-225 • The Nile, one of the world's greatest rivers, flows gently through its delta, creating wide coves.

225 • Near Luxor, great islands interrupt the Nile's flow, creating landscapes of ageless beauty.

226-227 • The Ain Umm Ahmed oasis, in Sinai, Egypt, offers primordial rock and sand landscapes.

● The Libyan Sahara shows unique colors
and forms, the fruit of millions of years of
geological and climactic phenomena. In
summer it is impossible to live in this habitat,
when the temperature usually reaches
about 158° F (70°C).

● A wide-ranging rain forest surrounds part of the Tanganyika basin, in Tanzania. This is one of the richest ecosystems of the world.

232-233 and 233 ● The Victoria Falls, on the Zambia-Zimbabwe border, expresses nature's raw power. A mile (1.5 km) in breadth, 426 ft (130 m) high, the falls are among the planet's most ravishing.

234-235 ● From the Tana River plain in Kenya one can see Kilimanjaro, which rises on the border with Tanzania. Kilimanjaro National Park protects the area and the peak, which in 1987 UNESCO designated as a World Heritage Site.

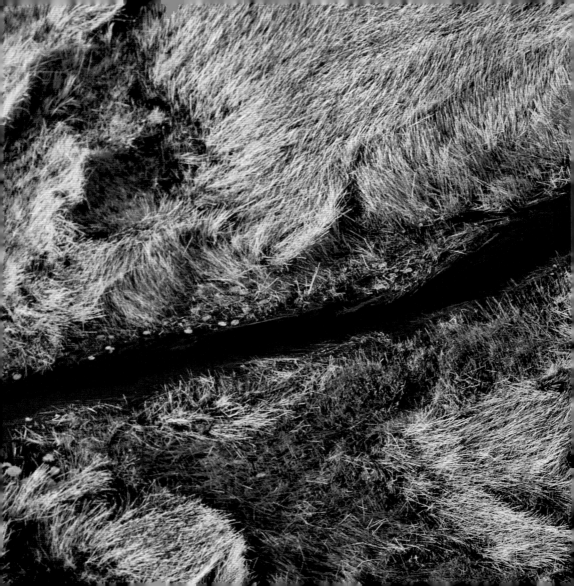

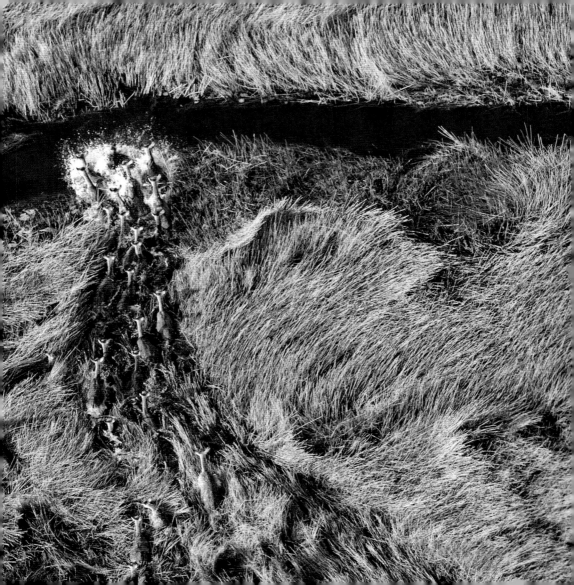

236-237 • The Masai Mara National Reserve is known for its outstanding wildlife and for the famous migration of gnus and zebras that takes place in October and April.

238-239 • From an environmental viewpoint, the Okavango River delta, in Botswana, is one of the world's most important wildlife areas. The delta was formed by colossal earthquakes that extended local river systems; it shelters many animals, such as these antelopes.

240 and 241 • Extending over 19,300 sq. miles (50,000 sq. km), the Namib-Naukluft National Park is Namibia's largest. The landscape varies from very high sand dunes to vast expanses of endless stony white and grey plains and to mountain massifs, deep canyons and ravines.

242-243 • Namibia's Sossusvlei area boasts the world's highest dunes, rising from 1800 to 1970 ft (550 to 600 m) above sea level.

244-245 • A colony of c. 1 million sea lions inhabits the Skeleton Coast, a stretch of the Namib Desert, in Namibia, which unfolds along the impressively desolate coast.

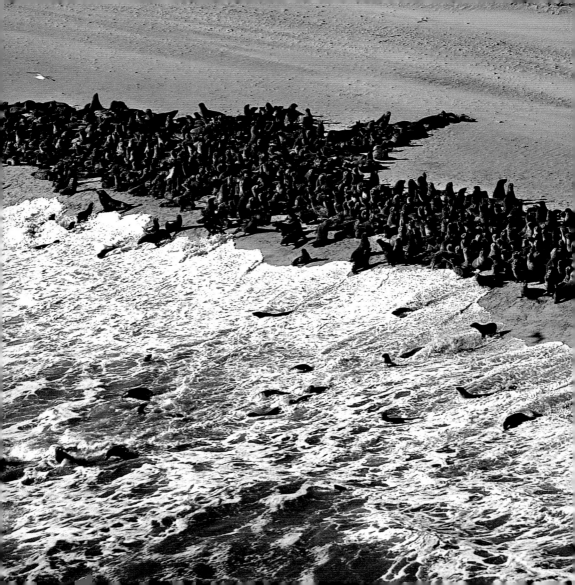

● White sand, crystal-clear seas and volcanic rocks eroded by tides and winds make a live postcard of Anse Source d'Argent, a beach on the island of La Digue, in the Seychelles.

Itsay National Park is a natural oasis located in north-central Madagascar. It is immersed in vegetation very similar to that of the Continental African savanna; great rocky formations rise, chiseled by the wind from the Isalo Roiniforme Massif.

250-251 • Tsingy de Bemaraha Reserve, in Madagascar, is characterized by sharp-pointed karstic formations, the so-called Tsingy, on which only lemurs manage to roam.

251 • Isalo is a massif of soft rock on which the action of the wind and erosion have created superb canyons, grottos and bizarre rock formations.

252-253 • The rock formations called "Fairy Chimneys," sculpted by the wind, are the heart of the National Park of Göreme, in Central Anatolia, Turkey, listed by UNESCO in 1985 as a World Heritage Site.

254-255 • Pamukkale (in Turkish meaning "cotton castle") owes its fame to the numberless thermal sources rich with hydrogen carbonate and calcium that color the mountain, forming terraces and white waterfalls that make the site precisely like a "cotton fortress."

The icons of the Maldives are the coconut tree, coral sands and transparent seas. A belt of coral reefs, safeguard all the islands of the archipelago and create the habitat for the multicolored tropical fish. Various canals cross the reefs, allowing the passage of the currents of the Indian Ocean, making the water of the atoll particularly life-sustaining.

258 and 258-259 ● If the eastern coast of Phi Phi Don is prevalently sandy, the west coast is characterized by majestically steep hills. Phi Phi Don is virtually subdivided into two islands connected by a thin strip of sand and vegetation.

260-261 ● The 19 lakes of Shuzeng and 18 of Nuorilang all fall under the protected area of Jiuzhaigou, in China: they resemble water terraces separated by calcareous formations that enclose colorful pools.

262-263 ● The Jiuzhaigou area, in China, possesses a complex hydrological system composed of countless rivers that flow into the Jialing, which in turn flows into the Yangtze. Waterfalls of enduring beauty course over multi-level terrain. The most famous waterfall is that of Zhengshutan, 0.8 miles (l.3 km) broad and 92 ft (28 m) high.

264 ● The Lijiang, the principal river of Guangxi province, China, flows slowly past steep karstic hills that rise unexpectedly from green fields and cultivated land.

265 ● The territory near Guilin is fascinating for the grandeur of its peaks and rock formations reflected in the rice fields. The landscape is one of the most fascinating in China.

266-267 • Seen from the glaciers, the southwest front of Mt Godwin-Austen (28,251 ft/8611 m), on the Chinese-Pakistan border, seems really inaccessible. The peak is also called K2, meaning the second highest summit in the Karakorum range, as inaccurately calculated in 1856.

268-269 • Mt Everest (29,029 ft/8848 m), on the Chinese-Nepalese border, dominates the Himalaya and the Kingdom of Eternal Snow. The peak's Tibetan name, Chomolangma (Mother of the Universe), captures its imposing grandeur.

270-271 • The sunrays at dusk strikingly illuminate Nuptse (25,791 ft/7861 m), in Nepal, one of the most stunning peaks framing Everest.

272 and 273 • Ama Dablam (22,493/6856 m), in Nepal, is seen here from two viewpoints; the name means "The Mother and her Necklace." Because of its shape, Ama Dablam is called the "Matterhorn of the Himalayas."

274-275 ● Cho Oyu (26,906 ft/8201 m) on the Chinese-Nepalese border, is the world's sixth highest peak. In Tibetan, Cho Oyu means "Turquoise Goddess."

275 ● Tibet is now an autonomous region of China, located on the plain often termed the Plateau of Tibet, at an average altitude of about 16,075 ft (4900 m). The landscape is both gentle and severe and also treeless because of its high altitude.

276-277 • The Danum Valley Conservation Area, in Sabah, Malaysia, is one of the world's very few remaining virgin forests. Sixty million years old, this rain forest in the heart of Malaysian Borneo hosts about 275 bird species and 110 mammal species.

278-279 • In the rice terraces that flank the Mekong in Vietnam, one can sense the fatigue of men and their buffaloes, immersed in water all day to be able to harvest a modest rice harvest from the hillsides.

● Halong Bay, in Vietnam, resembles
a great bewitched lagoon, with its
emerald-green waters, where three
thousand isles rise, like mountains
thrusting up to form a mythical landscape.

Mt Fuji (12,388/3776 m) is Japan's highest mountain. A sleeping volcano, its peak is snow-clad 10 months a year. Mt Fuji is a sacred symbol for the Japanese, who believe it is their duty to make a pilgrimage to its slopes at least once in their lifetime.

284 ● The fabulous island is one of the Whit Sunday Islands, off eastern Australia.

285 ● A sandy half-moon sprouts out from the waters of the Great Coral Reef off Australia.

286-287 ● The Great Coral Reef is the world's largest such phenomenon. Located far off the coast of Queensland, northeast Australia, it is a unique and fantastic environment. At some points the reef becomes a narrow strip of coral; at others it is 200 miles (320 km) in breadth.

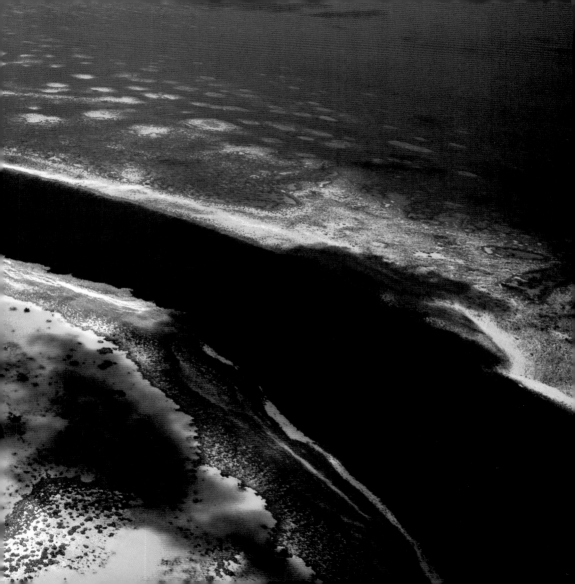

288 • The Kakadu National Park is one of Australia's most important natural protected areas; it has ecosystems richly diverse from one another, from the savanna to the famous Paperbark Swamp, whose marshes were formed by Magela Creek.

288-289 • The Kakadu National Park territory fenced in by the three channels of the Alligator River form a biological reserve basin also holding important minerals, such as uranium. The area is also famous for the presence of 1500 sites of aboriginal rock art..

290 • Uluru (also known as Ayers Rock) is one of Australia's almost universally known symbols. The gigantic red rock that rises from the desert owe its color to iron oxides and feldspar that reflects the sunlight.

290-291 • In the center of Uluru-Kata Tjuta National Park, in the heart of the Australian continent, rises the enormous monolith of Uluru, 1050 ft (320 m) high, with a diameter of 5 miles (8 km). For aborigines, Uluru is a sacred place.

● Aoraki/Mt Cook (12,313 ft/3753 m) is New Zealand's highest mountain. It is part of the Southern Alps chain, a sort of spinal column that runs along the west coast of Te Wai Pounamu, New Zealand's South Island.

294-295 • Seen here is the channel that connects the Mataiva lagoon, Tuamotu, with the ocean. The island is rich in phosphates but the inhabitants refused to allow their excavation because it would have altered the environmental equilibrium.

295 • The Tuamotu Archipelago includes at least 78 islands, forming a corner of Eden extending over 30,000 sq. miles (800,000 sq km) of the southern Pacific, but home to only 15,000 people.

296 and 297 ● Bora Bora is one of the Society Islands, French Polynesia. Surrounded by a lagoon and a ring of reefs, Bora Bora is famous for its transparent waters and for the wild panorama offered by its high peaks, covered by tropical vegetation. Above them towers the unmistakable Mt Otemanu, ancient legacy of an extinct volcano.

298-299 ● All the colors of the sea, from turquoise to cobalt blue, tint the sea around Mataiva, in the Tuamotu Archpelago, French Polynesia.

300-301 ● Bartolomé Island, in the Galápagos, off Ecuador, highlights the volcanic origin of the rock formations.

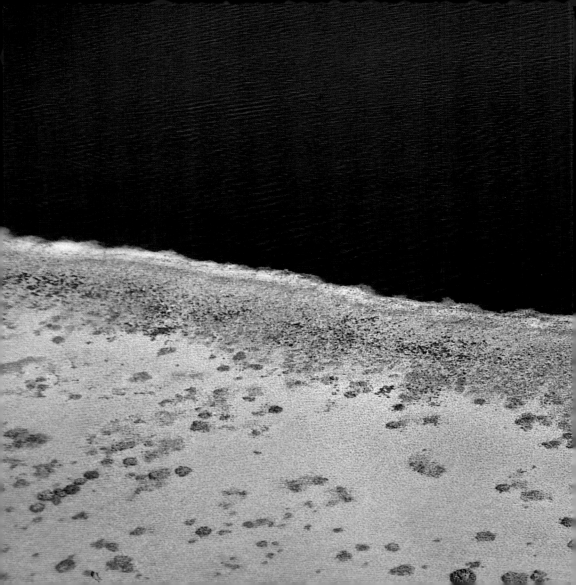

302-303 • The prehistoric land iguana, which can reach 6.5 ft (2 m), is the icon of the Galapagos Archipelago, which consists of 14 volcanic isles, some 620 miles (1000 km) off the coast of Ecuador.

304 and 304-305 •
The Canadian side of the Niagara Falls is a magnificent display of Nature's power. The Horseshoe Falls are so called because of the unmistakable "U" form of the rock lip.

For millennia, Yellowstone's Grand Canyon, Wyoming, U.S.A., has been excavated by the river of the same name. Two imposing waterfalls foam headlong over the yellow rock walls (from which the river's name is derived): the Lower Falls (seen here) and the Upper Falls.

308 ● The Merced River, which flows through the Yosemite Valley, California, U.S.A., is flanked by a small gem of a landscape.

309 ● A snow storm lashes out against El Capitan, the most renowned peak in Yosemite Valley, a vertical monolith (3000 ft/910 m) which challenges free climbers from all over the world.

310 • Monument Valley, on the Utah-Arizona border, is the icon of wild America: in the foreground are Stagecoach, Bear and Rabbit and Castle Rock, three of the most extraordinary rock formations called buttes.

311 • West Mitten Butte is also one of the famous scenic views that Monument Valley offers us.

312-313 • All of Earth's geological history is scripted on the wall of the Grand Canyon, Arizona, U.S.A.

314-315 • Composed of "tender" rock, the spires of Bryce Canyon, Utah, are subject to rapid erosion that gives life to this landscape which, covered with snow, assumes a fairy-tale atmosphere.

316 and 317 • Antelope Canyon, a place of breathtaking beauty located near Page, Arizona, is an unbelievable product of erosion.

318-319 • The highlands of Colorado are crossed by the Colorado river and its tributaries, winding streams that hollowed out deep canyons in the rocks.

● With unmistakable intensely green islands that seem to float like rafts in the deep blue sea, the Everglades, a subtropical marshy region in the south of Florida, U.S.A., is among the world's most outstanding humid zones.

● The fauna of the Everglades National Park includes Florida panthers (in the picture) along with eagles, flamingoes, pelicans, sea cows and of course, alligators which – only here – cohabit with crocodiles.

324 and 325 • The rainy season, which in Hawaii is very intense, is the cause of these amazing waterfalls.

326-327 • The spectacular fiery pit in Hawaii called Puu O'o came into being with the eruptions of Kilauea in 1983 and 1986.

● Of volcanic origin, just like the other islands of the Hawaiian Archipelago, Kauai is also the oldest and most mountainous. Despite its 50,000 inhabitants, a great part of the island is still a wild Eden, so much so that Steven Spielberg chose it as the location for his film, *Jurassic Park*.

● The island of Espiritu Santo, Mexico, in the Sea of Cortes with its vivid coast, where the ocher colors of its sandy shores dabble with the hues of the sea: turquoise near the shore, and cobalt blue offshore where it suddenly plummets down to abysmal depths.

● Snapshots of the lost Eden: the Agabama waterfalls in the Sierra del Escambray, Cuba, are the lymph for thousands of endemic vegetal species and for an especially rich tropical fauna. This part of the mountain chain which crosses the island's central region is protected by the Topes de Collantes natural reserve.

The Great Blue Hole, in Belize, is an impressive karstic underwater doline, almost perfectly round, in the Caribbean Sea. It is more than 984 ft (300 m) wide and 403 ft (123 m) deep; Jacques-Yves Cousteau chose it as one of the world's ten most interesting underwater sites.

336-337 • The Sarapiquí River, in Costa Rica, flows down from the historic Poás volcano, and then its course gathers speed in raging rapids, ending in fanciful waterfalls piercing through the green roof of the tropical forest.

338-339 • The Salto Angel Waterfall, in Venezuela, is the highest waterfall in the world (3212 ft/979 m). It cascades down into the Gran Savana from the highlands of the Auyantepui Mountain.

340-341 • The giant lotus: symbol of the Pantanal, a basin extending for 57,915 sq. miles (150,000 sq. km) over Brazil, Bolivia, and Paraguay. It is the world's largest humid zone.

342-343 • The Amazon River, in Brazil, slowly spreads out in many winding channels. During the rainy season the river course swells; in the dry season it is obstructed by the forest.

344-345 • The majestic Iguazú Falls on the Brazilian-Argentinian border comprise 300 falls extending almost 1.8 miles (3 km) in width and reaching 230 ft (70 m) in height.

346-347 • Bounded by the Andes and the ocean, 350,000 sq. miles (900,000 sq. km) of desert, plain, and highlands extends from the Rio Colorado to Tierra del Fuego, Patagonia, with its c. 2.2 inhabitants per sq. km.

348-349 • The Andean Cordillera encompasses some of the world's most stunning glaciers. Among them the Perito Moreno, in Argentina, extending over about 155 sq. miles (300 sq. km), is one of few still expanding glaciers.

350-351 • Huascarán, in the Cordillera Blanca, Argentina, is part of a chain of amazing and inaccessible ice peaks. The Cordillera, 112 miles (180 km) in length, is composed of 50 peaks over 18,700 ft (5700 m), and includes the great Parco Nacional del Huascarán, opened in 1975.

352-353 ● Even if not among the highest Andean peaks, Cerro Fitzroy, on the Argentinean-Chilean frontier, is a world famous icon. The massif, of incomparable beauty and towering at 11,171 ft (3405 m) like a rock cathedral, is an extremely difficult climbing challenge.

354-355 ● The Cordillera del Paine is a small but spectacular mountain chain in the Torres del Paine National Park, in Chile's Patagonia. Seen from glacial Lake Pehoe, the three Cuernos del Paine – the Norte, the Principal and the Este – rise in the center of the picture.

356 • Snow and floating glaciers inhabit the splendid Paradise Bay, in Antarctica, walled in by low snow-capped mountains.

357 • Fragments of icebergs seem to follow the road traced out by the clouds at sunset, on a summer evening at Holtedehl Bay, Antarctica.

358-359 • Summer in Antarctica: the pack splits into three enormous slabs, but the icebergs still remain majestic ice mountains.

360-361 • The Emperor penguins live in dense colonies and conduct an intense family life. They are the most outstanding symbols of Antarctica.

362-363 • The proportions of this monumental iceberg are evident. But history has recorded even bigger formations; Iceberg B-15, which during year 2000 detached from the Ross Ices Shelf, Antarctica, had a surface area of 4250 sq. miles (11,000 sq. km); the largest on record.

The SIGNS of MAN

FEDERICA ROMAGNOLI

- The setting sun paints the surface of the metallic skin that covers the structure of the Guggenheim Museum, Bilbao, Spain, designed by Frank Gehry.

INTRODUCTION The Signs of Man

STONE SPIRES PROUDLY STANDING OUT AGAINST THE SKIES AND MODERN BUILDINGS WITH TRANSPARENT GLASS SURFACES REFLECTING THE CLOUDS AND DOMES THAT SEEM TO FLOAT IN THE AIR; BRIDGES WITH SLENDER ARCHES REACHING UP TOWARD THE INFINITE, FORESTS OF COLUMNS LIKE STALAGMITES AND GOLDEN ROOFS SHINING IN THE EASTERN SUN – THIS VOLUME IS AN ANTHOLOGY OF EXTRAORDINARY IMAGES, A JOURNEY THROUGH TIME AND SPACE TO MEET SOME OF THE MOST BEAUTIFUL ARCHITECTURE OF OUR PLANET.

THIS IS ARCHITECTURE THAT GOES WELL BEYOND OFFERING SIMPLE ANSWERS TO HUMANKIND'S PRIMARY NEED OF CREATING ADEQUATE ROOFED SPACE UNDER WHICH TO SHELTER AND LIVE, BUT WHICH ALSO ACCOMPLISHES A SERIES OF FURTHER FUNCTIONS.

INTRODUCTION The Signs of Man

VITRUVIUS ALREADY CONSIDERED SOLIDITY *(FIRMITAS)*, USEFUL-
NESS *(UTILITAS)* AND BEAUTY *(VENUSTAS)* AS THE THREE PRE-
REQUISITES ESSENTIAL TO EVERY BUILDING, AND THESE ELE-
MENTS ARE FOUND IN ALL THE MASTERPIECES ILLUSTRATED IN
THESE PAGES, MANY OF WHICH HAVE MARKED THEIR SITES FOR
CENTURIES WITH THEIR UNMISTAKABLE PRESENCE. THESE SOL-
ID MASSES OF STONE – AWE-INSPIRING SYMBOLS OF GRAND EU-
ROPEAN CITIES SUCH AS LONDON AND PARIS, ARE BALANCED
BY THE LIGHTNESS AND TRANSPARENCY OF MORE RECENT AR-
CHITECTURE: FUTURISTIC MUSEUMS, CULTURAL CENTERS AND
PUBLIC BUILDINGS. THE MAGICAL ATMOSPHERE OF SPAIN –
FROM THE ARABIC FASCINATION OF THE ALHAMBRA TO THE VI-
SIONARY GAUDÍ, FROM THE TORTUOUS FORMS OF GEHRY TO
THE ORGANIC AND FUTURISTIC ONES OF CALATRAVA – AND THE

The Signs of Man
Introduction

SOLEMN MAJESTY OF THE MOST RENOWNED ITALIAN CATHE-
DRALS COMPLETE THE PICTURE OF THE WONDERS OF THE OLD
CONTINENT. TOWARD THE EAST, IN TURKEY AND RUSSIA, FROM
AMONG THE DOMES AND MINARETS, THE FIRST ECHOES OF THE
ORIENT CAN BE HEARD, ALMOST LIKE HERALDS, ANNOUNCING
THE OSTENTATIOUS MAGNIFICENCE OF ASIA'S TEMPLES AND
PALACES, THE BEAUTY OF WHICH TODAY IS RIVALED BY THE
DIZZYING HEIGHTS OF MODERN BUILDINGS, THEIR SHAPES OF-
TEN INSPIRED BY TRADITION. AND TO FOLLOW, AMERICA, THE
SYMBOL OF MODERNIZATION AND THE HISTORIC BIRTHPLACE
OF THE SKYSCRAPER, AND THEN THE MAGICAL SAILS OF THE
OPERA HOUSE IN SYDNEY, SOARING UP TOWARD THE AUS-
TRALIAN SKIES.

- This view of Haghia Sophia, which Emperor Justinian commissioned and built in Istanbul during the 6th century, highlights its complexity and stateliness.

The HSB Turning Torso Tower designed by Santiago Calatrava is the highest residential tower in Sweden; its 623 ft (190 m) dominate Malmö's horizontal landscape.

372 • London's Tower Bridge was built between 1886 and 1894 according to the project design of Horace Jones and John W. Barry.

372-373 • The colors decorating Tower Bridge – white, blue and red – are those of the British flag.

374-375 • Westminster Palace, seat
of the British Parliament, with the Big Ben
clock tower rising nearby.

375 • Victoria Tower is 336 ft (102.5 m)
tall; it houses the Parliamentary Archives.

30 St Mary Axe, nicknamed "the Gherkin," is one of the most recognizable features of the British capital's skyline.

378 ● A flock of sheep graze in the fields surrounding Mont Saint-Michel, in Normandy, dominated by the Benedictine Abbey dedicated to St. Michael Archangel.

379 ● At high tide, the hill becomes a little island, linked to the mainland only by an access road that is protected by a dam.

❋ Chenonceaux,
situated inside a big
park, is one of the Loire
Valley's most charming
châteaux. It was built
in the 16th century,
incorporating a five-
arched bridge spanning
the River Cher.

- Francis I, who bought
  Chambord in 1519,
  transformed the
  modest hunting lodge
  of the Counts of Blois
  into an immense
  complex of 440 rooms,
  the biggest château
  in the Loire Valley.

Elegant geometrical figures characterize the gardens of the Château de Villandry, in the Loire Valley. It was largely rebuilt in the 20th century on the basis of the 16th-century plans of Jacques Androuet du Cerceau the Elder. Inside the Renaissance building is a square medieval tower, legacy of the fort that used to stand on the original site.

● The impressive château of Chaumont, overlooking the Loire, was rebuilt between the end of the Middle Ages and the start of the 16th century by the counts d'Amboise. Like most Loire châteaux, it has noteworthy collections of furniture tapestry and objets d'art of various eras.

The Cathedral of Notre Dame, in Paris, is one of the monuments of Gothic architecture. Construction began in 1163, commissioned by Maurice de Sully. The main façade, facing west and dominated by two towers, is structured with notable compositional accuracy, cradling in its center a splendid Rose Window with polychromatic glass.

● Since 1889, engineer Gustave Eiffel's iron tower has dominated the French capital. It was to have been dismantled after the Universal Expo, but significant prospective uses saved it from destruction.

● The arched base of the Eiffel Tower, the metallic framework of which is lighted up at night, focuses on the solemn façade of the Éccle Militaire.

● In the Versailles Palace gardens, designed by André Le Nôtre for Louis XIV, the "Sun King", a complex irrigation system allowed for the creation of a series of pools, composed of large basins decorated with groups of bronze statues.

● A fable-like
atmosphere envelops
Neuschwanstein
Castle, in the Bavarian
Alps. Commissioned
by King Ludwig II
of Bavaria, it was built
between 1868
and 1886.

Starting off from the lantern on top of the cupola of the Reichstag in Berlin, designed by Norman Foster, a helicoidal staircase leads to a platform where one can see into the hall of the Parliament, the Bundestag.

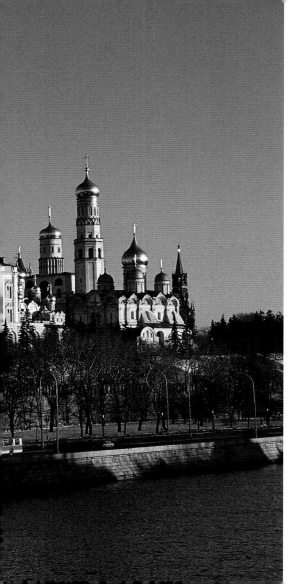

The impressive mass of the Grand Kremlin Palace acts as a golden framework and towers that challenge the skies. The building, designed by Konstantin Thon and completed in 1849, looks out on the Moscow River, which runs through the city.

● In the past, Moscow's Cathedral of the Dormition, with its richly frescoed interior, was the coronation site of Russa's sovereigns.

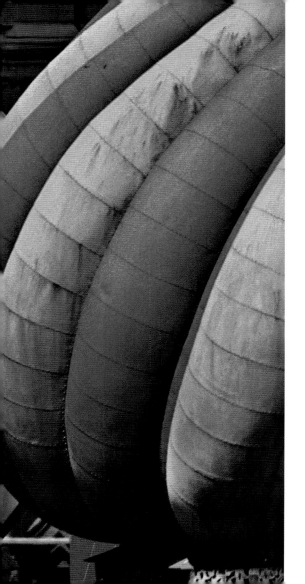

404-405 ● The vividly colored onion- or bulb-shaped domes of St. Basil's Cathedral, in Moscow, date back to the end of the 16th century.

405 ● The Cathedral of the Annunciation, in Moscow, with its sensational golden domes, was rebuilt after a fire destroyed it in 1547.

● The Patio of the
Lions, constructed
in the 16th century
as part of the Alhambra
complex in Granada,
is a refined Moorish-
style structure with
a mass of subtle
columns.

● The sensational engravings of the fragile *muquarnas*, "stalactite" elements created with stucco, confer an extraordinary richness on the decorative ornaments of the Alhambra, Granada.

In this picture taken from Mirador de San Nicolás in the Albayzín quarter, the Alhambra, whose imposing tower dominates the majestic panorama of Granada, is framed by the white peaks of the Sierra Nevada.

411

412 • Brightly colored ceramics decorate the finials of the dizzying towers of the Sagrada Família, the basilica which serves the symbol of Barcelona. It was designed by the Catalan architect Antoni Gaudí.

413 • The main characteristic of the Sagrada Família is its forceful vertical development, here seen from the side of the Nativity, the only one Gaudí managed to finish before his death. The building is still incomplete.

Some stone sculptures with intense and troubled expressions adorn the Sagrada Família such as those decorating the façade of the Passion, to the west, where the sculpture group portraying the Passion of Christ stands. Designed by Josep Maria Subirachs, it was completed toward the end of the 20th century.

416 ● Valencia's City of Art and Science, designed by Santiago Calatrava, is a vast complex dedicated to culture and science within which futuristic buildings stand.

417 ● The Oceanographic Park Auditorium of Valencia was built in 2001 and is recognizable for its soaring roofs designed by Félix Candela (1910-1997).

● The Tenerife Opera House, designed by Santiago Calatrava, thrusts itself in all its clear-cut beauty into the pink Canarian sky. The light reflects on the white ceramic finishing that covers and confers marine hues to the plastic form hanging over it, very much like a wing or a powerful wave.

419

These aerial views from Platea Marciana, the civil and religious heart of Venice, offer two different glimpses of Piazza San Marco and the Basilica of the same name with its five big domes and the Palazzo Ducale facing the Piazzetta and the Riva degli Schiavoni.

• The façade of the Basilica of St Mark, in Venice, shines with its lively polychromatic mosaics on a golden background, all restructured, except one – between the 17th and the 19th centuries, following the basic original designs.

A warm and suffused light, that changes with the hour of day, enfolds the precious decorations of mosaic art on a golden background depicting Bible stories that cover the wall, the vaults and the domes of the Basilica of St Mark, extending over a surface of 86,110 sq. ft (8000 sq. m).

426-427 • On the green clearing of the Field of Miracles, in Pisa, is the cathedral in Pisan-Romanic style, consecrated in 1118 but completed around the middle of the 12th century.

427 • Santa Maria del Fiore Cathedral, the imposing dome with eight gores, in Florence, was built in the 15th century by Filippo Brunelleschi, whereas its Bell Tower had been designed by Giotto just a century earlier.

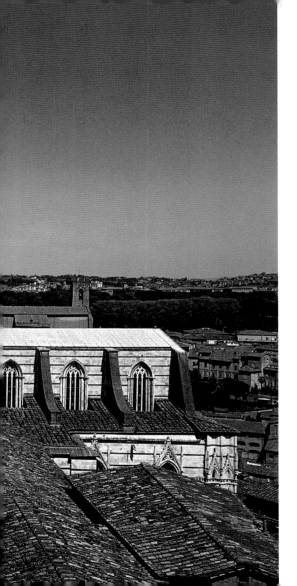

The unmistakable tower with black and white horizontal lines shoots up from Siena's Cathedral, a masterpiece of Romanic-Gothic architecture from the second half of the 12th century, completed at the end of the 14th century.

● The grandeur of Gian Lorenzo Bernini's colonnade, designed in 1656 and crowned by 96 statues, stand like a decorative frame for St Peter's Basilica, where many important 17th-century architects had worked, such as Carlo Maderno who in 1614 completed the façade.

The Alexandrian Library,
Egypt, designed by the
Norwegian master Snohetta,
is a big cylinder obliquely refinished
with glass panels, making it
resemble a great inclined sun
arising from the waters.

● Abu Dhabi Investment Authority Tower
(ADIA), built in 2007, was designed by the
architectural company of Kohn Pedersen
Fox. With its 38 floors, it is a dramatic
feature of the Abu Dhabi skyline, in the
United Emirates.

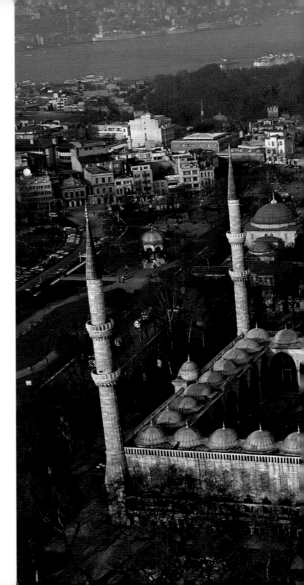

436 ● The Mosque of Suleiman I, in Istanbul, was built by the architect Sinan between 1550 and 1557.

436-437 ● Istanbul's Blue Mosque, which was built between 1609 and 1616, has six polygonal minarets. In the background, the reddish mass of Haghia Sophia dominates the Bosporus.

● The Blue Mosque
owes its name to the
color of the fantastic
majolica from Iznik.
It is painted with flower
designs that cover the
walls of the main hall.

● In the center of the Temple Esplanade, in Jerusalem, stands the Dome of the Rock, with its characteristic octagonal form. Building started in 685, during the Umayyad era (661-750).

442 • A glimpse of the dome of the Gur-é Amir, Samarkand, from behind a minaret. The mausoleum was built between 1398 and 1404.

442-443 • The Tilya-Kori Madrasah rises at the north end of the Registan, "the sandy place" of Samarkand, Uzbekistan.

444-445 • The Tilya-Kori Madrasah of Samarkand was built between 1647 and 1660 by order of the city governor Yalangtush Bahadur.

● The Taj Mahal, in Agra, radiates splendor. The mausoleum was commissioned by Shah Jahan in memory of his beloved wife Mumtaz Mahal, and built between 1631 and 1648. The mausoleum stands on a raised base, with minarets at the four corners.

448-449 and 449 • Flanking the Taj Mahal are two red tuff mosques, each with a dome with gores in white marble, decorated on the inside with typical Muslim-inspired naturalistic geometric designs.

450-451 • The fortress at Amber, on the banks of Lake Maota, near Jaipur, Rajasthan, was transformed into a royal residence in the 17th century.

Today Amber fortress-residence is one of the most beautiful Indian palaces. Its Sattais Katcheri (left) colonnade is remarkable for its 27 elegant pillars.

● The Hava Mahal or "Wind Palace" in Jaipur, India, built in 1799 by Maharaja Sawai Pratap Singh, is a striking five-story construction seemingly made of pinkish sand. Looking through the filigree window gratings, the women of the royal household could see – without being seen – the intense life that unfolded in the city streets.

Construction of the complex of buildings that form the Grand, or Royal, Palace in Bangkok, Thailand, started in 1782 during the reign of King Rama I. The complex includes a variety of buildings, among which the most important is the octagonal gold-tiled chedi, the Phra Sri Ratana.

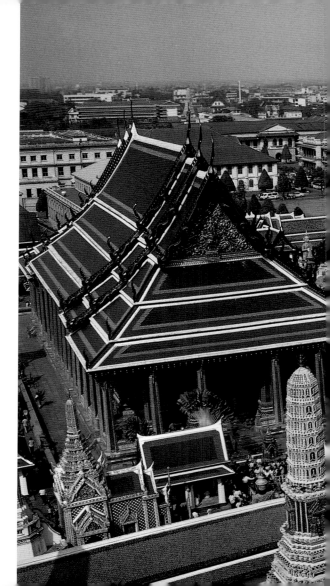

Golden Hues in
a Celebration
of Colors

● The statues and the elaborate decorations that enhance
the Wat Phra Kaew or "Temple of the Emerald Buddha,"
in the Grand Palace of Bangkok, portray appliqué and
sculpted motifs in relief, with bright colors, like in this
personified green yaksha (right).

• The Potala rises on the slopes of the Marpori, or Red Mountain, outside Lhasa, Tibet.

462-463 ● Two bucks facing one another with the "wheel of the Dharma" between them. This symbol of the Buddhist religion decorates the pavilion of the Jokhang Temple, in Lhasa.

463 ● Fierce snow lions adorn the many sacred buildings of Tibet.

464 • This bronze lioness guards the Taihemen, or Door of Supreme Harmony, in the Forbidden City, in Beijing.

464-465 • The Shenwumen, the Door of Divine Military Power, closes the north end of the immense complex.

466 ● The corners of the roofs of imperial buildings are decorated with groups of Chinese mythical animals in glazed ceramics.

466-467 ● The Zhonghedian, the Hall of Central Harmony, on the right, stands near the Baohedian, the Hall of Preserved Harmony.

China's frenzied race toward economic development is well represented by Shanghai's Jin Mao Tower, rising 1381 ft (421 m) in the Pudong district.

The skyline of Kuala Lumpur, in Malaysia, which features the unmistakable Petronas Towers designed by Cesar Pelli, displays an evident revival of the typical forms of Far Eastern religious architecture.

- The Kansai International Airport terminal, near Osaka, in Japan, was designed by Renzo Piano and constructed between 1988 and 1994. It stands on an artificial island 3 miles (5 km) away from the mainland.

474-475 ✴ Himeji Castle, with its gently curved roofs, was erected in the 14th century in Harima province, Japan. A majestic country house, rebuilt in 1577, lies immersed in the greenery of the pine trees.

476-477 ✴ The magnificent sails of Sydney's Opera House, in Sydney, stand out in the warm light of the sunset. The building was designed by the Danish Jørn Utzon during the 1950s.

478-479 ✴ The original structure conceived by Renzo Piano for the Cultural Center of Tjibaou, in Nouméa Bay, New Caledonia harmoniously blends with the surrounding environment.

● Designed by William van Alen in the late 1920s and completed in 1930, the Chrysler Building in New York displays a tapering figure and splendid finish in chromium-plated steel with décor elements inspired by automobile designs of the era.

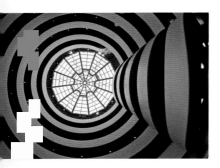

The Guggenheim Museum in New York, built toward the end of the 1950s, was conceived by Frank Lloyd Wright as a continuum of surfaces that accompanies the visitors immersing themselves in the world of art, as in a symphony.

ER COLLECTION

S O L O M O N R G U G G E N H E I M M U S E

- The Statue of Liberty, a gift of the French people to the Americans, stands on Liberty Island and since 1886 has welcomed those who arrive in New York by sea. Edouard de Laboulaye designed the statue, but the sculptor who created it was Frédéric Auguste Bartholdi.

● The Empire State Building – one of the symbols of New York – soars up to an
impressive height of 1250 ft (381 m) (higher if the antenna is included), a truly
extraordinary achievement for the 1930s.

The dark-toned John Hancock Center, one of the Chicago skyline's most representative buildings, rises to a vertiginous height of 1129 ft (344 m). This steel-and-glass giant, designed by SOM, is often called "Big John."

490 ● The top of one of the red towers of the Golden Gate, San Francisco's most acclaimed bridge, high above the blue waters of the strait that carries the city's name.

490-491 ● Low clouds cover part of the 4200-ft (1280-m) central span of the Golden Gate Bridge.

492 • A sculpture depicting the face of Brasilian President Juscelino Kubitschek, who in 1956 launched the bid for the planning of the new capital. His statue watches over the Supreme Court of Justice.

493 • The bronze statues of the four Evangelists at the entrance of the Metropolitan Cathedral of Brasilia seem almost as if they wished to protect the faithful entering this unusual structure designed by Oscar Niemeyer and built between 1958 and 1970.

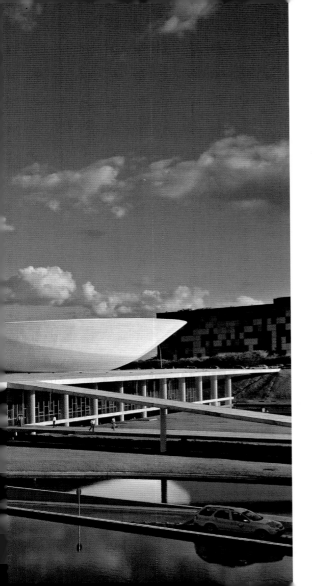

494-495 ● The towers of Brazil's Parliament building dominate the dome of the Chamber of Deputies and that – inverted – of the Senate.

495 ● Like the Parliament, the Itamaraty Palace in Brasilia was designed by Oscar Niemeyer. It houses the Ministry of Foreign Affairs.

The statue of Christ the Redeemer, 98 ft (30 m) tall, looks down on Rio de Janeiro from the summit of the Corcovado, 2330 ft (710 m) high. The statue was created by a group of artisans headed by the French sculptor Paul Landowski.

Valeria Manferto De Fabianis, the editor of the series, was born in Vercelli, Italy, and studied arts at the Università Cattolica del Sacro Cuore in Milan, graduating with a degree in philosophy. She is an enthusiastic traveler and nature lover. She has collaborated on the production of television documentaries and articles for the most prestigious Italian specialty magazines and has also written the text for many photography books. She co-founded Edizioni White Star in 1984 with Marcello Bertinetti and is the editorial director.

INDEX

The texts are by **Alberto Bertolazzi**, **Giorgio Ferrero**, and **Federica Romagnoli**. Alberto Bertolazzi studied philosophy at the University of Pavia. After teaching for a brief period, he started writing for Italian newspapers and periodicals. He worked for White Star Publishers on the production of the books *Lisbon* (1997) and *Portugal* (1998), and has written the text for many other titles on nature. Giorgio Ferrero studied classic literature at the University of Milan and wrote his thesis on Egyptology. He has since worked in publishing, currently for White Star Publishers for whom he wrote *Egypt – the History and Treasures of an Ancient Civilization*. Federica Romagnoli obtained a Ph.D. in Indian and Far Eastern art history from the University of Genoa in 1995. For White Star Publishers she has written *Ancient China – the History and Treasures of an Ancient Civilization*, as well as contributing to the publication of a great number of works on architecture and the Far East.

PHOTO CREDITS

PHOTO CREDITS

● A *kinnara*, an Indian centaur, engraved on a 2nd century BC relief, Bodh Gaya, India.